United States Coast Guard

by Julie Murray

ABDO
U.S. ARMED FORCES
Kids

www.abdopublishing.com

Published by Abdo Kids, a division of ABDO, PO Box 398166, Minneapolis, Minnesota 55439.

Copyright © 2015 by Abdo Consulting Group, Inc. International copyrights reserved in all countries. No part of this book may be reproduced in any form without written permission from the publisher.

Printed in the United States of America, North Mankato, Minnesota.

052014

092014

Photo Credits: Alamy, Corbis, Getty Images, Shutterstock, Thinkstock, © U.S. Coast Guard p.13, © TSgt Michael Holzworth p.19, © Steve Collender p.1 / © Gary Blakeley p.5 / © Ivan Cholakov p.11 / © RCPPHOTO p.15 / Shutterstock.com

Production Contributors: Teddy Borth, Jennie Forsberg, Grace Hansen

Design Contributors: Candice Keimig, Laura Rask, Dorothy Toth

Library of Congress Control Number: 2013953955

Cataloging-in-Publication Data

Murray, Julie.

 United States Coast Guard / Julie Murray.

   p. cm. -- (U.S. Armed Forces)

ISBN 978-1-62970-095-3 (lib. bdg.)

Includes bibliographical references and index.

1. United States Coast Guard--Juvenile literature.   I. Title.

363.28--dc23

                    2013953955

Table of Contents

United States Coast Guard

The Coast Guard is a branch

of the U.S. **Armed Forces**.

The Coast Guard keeps the waters safe. They also help in **emergencies**. They help in hurricanes and floods.

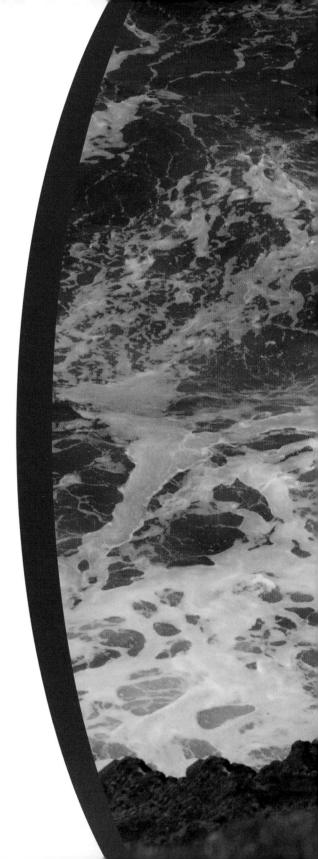

The Coast Guard searches for lost boats. They also rescue people **stranded** at sea.

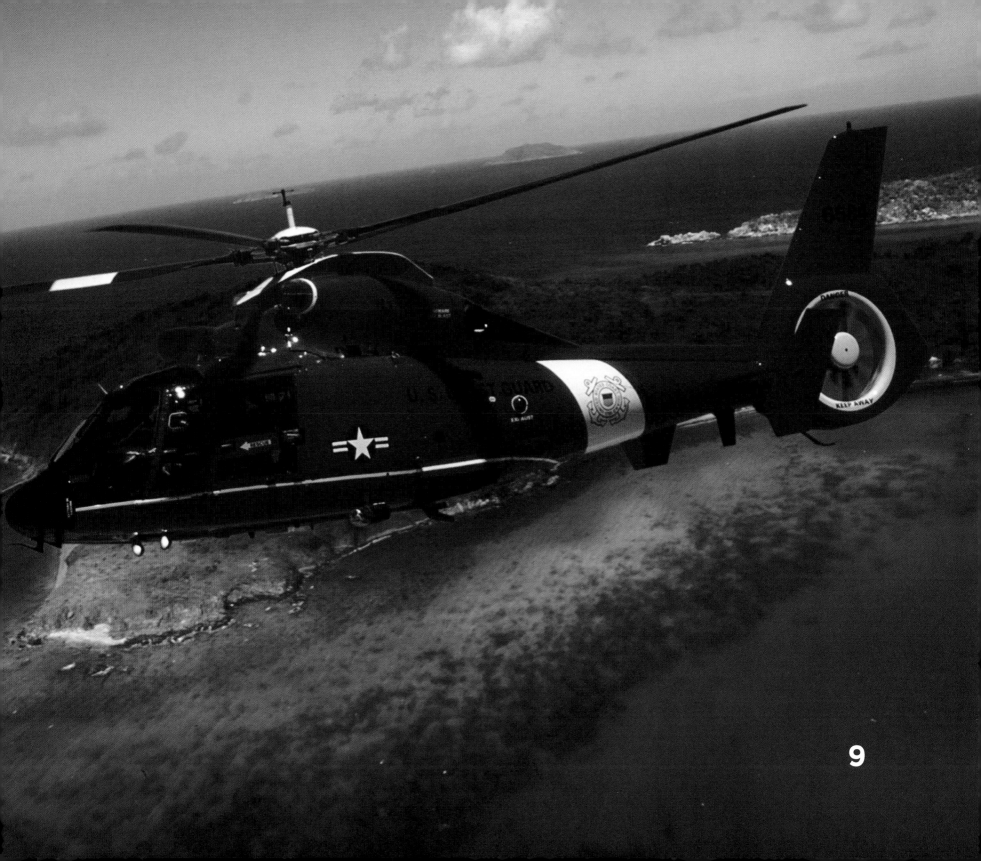

9

Vehicles

The Coast Guard uses large

boats. They are called cutters.

87312   U.S. COAST GUARD

Icebreak **cutters** help ships
go through icy waters safely.

The Coast Guard also uses smaller boats. They use helicopters and airplanes too.

Jobs

There are many jobs in the Coast Guard. Gunner's mates work with weapons.

Storekeepers keep track of supplies. Pilots fly planes and helicopters.

"*Semper Paratus*"

The Coast Guard keeps

Americans safe every day!